Supernovae

David Vidales

Supernovae

DEDICATION

My last few months have been far from perfect, and I made some mistakes but no matter what, this amazing person never judged me, never disappointed in my decisions, and was and is always there for me no matter what. Tanisha, I love you more then you know. When the universe made our paths cross, I never thought in a million years I would be getting a best friend, a sister, and a lifelong person.

ACKNOWLEDGMENTS

I would like to first express a special thank you to a small group of people always there giving me feedback. Every single one of you stood by me in these last few months when tragedy and heartache consumed and nearly ended me. Everything in my life at that point was truly a test and challenge, within a blink of an eye everything no longer existed. Having such amazing friends some I have never met, yet their compassion and love is unlike anything I have ever felt. Thank you all so very much, I will never be able to show you all how profoundly grateful I am. To my seven reasons why, I love you all so much, you all have helped make me the dad and man.

FOR KRYSTLE

SHROUDED IN MYSTERY SUCH AS
THE OCEANS DEPTH, SWORN OFF
LOVE ONLY NOW BUT A WORD;
AROUND HER HEART YOU MIGHT

NOT SEE A FORTRESS SO LOVE SHE CAN NOW DEFLECT. A
STAR SLOWLY DIMS BEFORE GOING SUPERNOVA, IN HER EYES
YOU CAN WITNESS SUCH FORCE; PAST LOVE AND HURT SET IN
MOTION HER COSMIC EXPLOSION.

FRAGMENTS FROM HER HEART,
COSMIC DUST FROM HER SOUL; FEW
HAVE WITNESSED THIS BEAUTY
FALL APART. WHAT YOU WILL
NOT SEE, AND FEW ONLY
KNOW, WITH THE DEATH OF ALL
THAT HURT

THOSE PARTICLES, FRAGMENTS AND COSMIC DUST; WILL SOON
FORM AND CREATE A BRIGHTER STRONGER SOUL WHICH WILL
SHINE BRIGHTER THAN BEFORE.

WHEN I WAS

When I was saying good night, you were figuring out which movie to watch together. When I was saying good morning, you were making him breakfast. When I asked you if you ate, you had just stopped for lunch for you two. When I asked how your day was and you replied boring, yet in the back of your mind you replayed your days

adventures. When you asked me if I was fine, I faked it and said I will be. Crushing me destroying me never even thinking of anyone else's feelings but your own. What goes around comes around, I am not mad or upset I am hurt I allowed it to happen again, knowing I knew all the signs.

TERMINAL LOVE

That dreadful day will forever play, the unspeakable things I never

thought you would

say. Leaving my

heart once again

shattered, today I

slowly started

picking up those

pieces. With each jagged

edge trying to understand, I see our loving memories dripping red off

my hands. Tears falling down my face yet smiling at all the memories

we were able to create. Remembering that beautiful day, we first met;

oh the smile on your face will be forever on repeat. They say

sometimes forever lasts only one second, our one second will forever

be a beautiful essence.

IF YOU'RE ASKING

If you are asking if I need you, the answer is no. If you are asking if I will always be there for you, the is answer not anymore. If you are asking if I still care and worry about you, the answer is I used to. If you are asking if I still think of you, the answer is I cannot remember the last time you crossed my mind. If you are asking if I still love you.... The question is did you ever really love me?

SAD TRUTH

As sad as this sounds, I will never give up hope of you coming home. Back to these arms that you once held, making you feel safe and always ready to defend. Still to this day so many questions I have, how did this happen; why you could not just tell me. You left with no warning, not even a note, no words even spoke. It keeps me up at night, hoping that you are ok, asking myself daily I wonder if you ate; we both know your memory I use to tease often. Are you sad and lonely too or have you completely forgot about me? Do I cross your mind, like you do every minute of mine?

A BROKEN PROMISES

Promises have been made with carefully spoken words. My secrets were shared, some have never been spoken. Trusting you with bits of my fragile past, you promises this would be the last. That was my own fault you made me think you were different. Finally my pieces you picked up shaping and sculpturing to your liking. To you it was merely a game you would eventually get tired of. I know now I was nothing to you but a child's toy. Bored you became no longer would I be a spark in your interest. As an old damaged toy, throwing me aside, finding something used and dull to your liking.

AS I SIT BACK

AS I SIT BACK FROM AFAR WATCHING YOU DRAG ME THROUGH THE MUD. KNOWING NOT TOO LONG AGO I WAS THE MAN YOU ONCE LOVED. I TOLD YOU MY SECRETS OF SO MANY IN THE PAST, BEGGING YOU NOT TO DO FOLLOW IN THEIR TRACKS. SPENDING OUR DAYS LOST IN WORDS, BELIEVING WE WERE SOULMATES OF THIS BLINDFOLDED LOVE. WAS IT YOUR PLAN RIGHT FROM THE START, FOR CHILD'S PLAY WITH ANOTHER MAN'S HEART?

DISTANCE DID NOT HELP THE MATTER I WAS ALWAYS LONELY ON MY CHILLY WINTER NIGHTS, WHILE YOU WERE BEING KEPT WARM FROM A MAN WHO AT THE TIME WOULD SUFFICE. JUST AS FAST AS THIS LOVE BEGIN TO BLOOM YOU RIPPED OFF THE LOVE BLINDFOLD REVEALING ALL TO SEE YOUR HIDDEN SCHEME. PLACING ME WITH ALL THE BLAME UNABLE TO DEFEND OR EVEN EXPLAIN, HOW I WAS PLAYED UP UNTIL THAT VERY DAY. THE VICTIM'S CARD YOU PLAY TODAY, PORTRAYING ME TO BE THE MONSTER OF THE WHOLE THING. DESTROYED AND CRUSHED WITH A NEWFOUND PAIN, INJECTING MY SOUL WITH YOUR CALMING AND LOVING TOUCH. COURSING THROUGH MY VEINS AS YOUR VENOM SLOWLY DECAYED, LIKE A CANCER SILENTLY EATING MY SOUL AWAY. MY ONCE UNTOUCHED SOUL ALMOST DEAD TODAY AS YOU STAND OVER STALKING YOUR PREY. YOU HAVE DRAINED MY ONCE VIBRANT LIFE, LEAVING NOTHING BUT EMPTY INSIDE.

FATES MISTAKE

Fate made a master plan, bringing two star crossed lovers together after a life span. The sparkle in her eyes, now brighter than the stars in the sky. His love for her unlike any ever seen on earth, now she knows all that she is worth. Unlike fairytale love written so long before, this once true love will be nevermore. The glance in her eyes such hurt she hides; her now fake smile is what she provides. The fire once burning deep inside, has now flickered, and died. Star crossed lovers destined to be, but no love in this world is what it is really meant to be.

TIME HEALS ALL PAIN

They say time heals all pain, heartbroken never saw it coming, gave everything type love. The love you only read about in books, could two people really have that love, share that love, feel that love and know that love. No, no one can love like that, love is a mystery such as the Bermuda Triangle we do not know why it exist, or how but it does it just exist. When we get such a small taste for it, we crave it like a new addiction; we do not know why we just do. Love is such a tangled mess of used lines, left over lies and hurtful phrases and uncertainty. Maybe one day love will make sense, but then again do we really want it to make sense

NO LONGER

I will tell you this, no longer will I search for love. I do not have time to sit idling by waiting to see if she could ever have any feelings for this man let alone love. I want love to come to me like the words of a poem. Delicately ready to be laid out, its newly fresh canvas will be forever. Slowly and softly intertwining as one. No jagged edges, nor bends not damaged layers. Slowly they meet their fate now in command. The letters being the only thing forever binding and forging as one this eternal love that will last way beyond the worlds end.

MY NEW NIGHTMARES

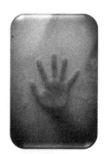

ONCE YOU WERE MY DREAM, COMING TO ME ON MY DARKEST NIGHTS. CALMING MY DEMONS, SILENCING MY ENDLESS SCARES. HOLDING ME TELLING ME YOU WERE THERE, EVEN WHEN YOUR PRESENCE WAS NOT FELT. THOSE DAYS ARE GONE, MY NIGHTMARES HAVE NOW RETURNED NO LONGER MY DEMONS HAUNT ME; YOUR IMAGES AND MEMORIES ARE MY NEW NIGHT TERRORS.

NONE OF THIS WAS EVER PLANNED

From the first time I held her hand, knowing that this was never planned. Falling for her soul before our eyes could meet, her soft tinder lips ever so sweet. Talk that went into the early morning, just the sound of her voice so adoring. Random silly goofy acts, never caring who saw the uncontrollable laughs. Finally finding someone who truly got me, running our own little world her and I were so free. The talks have drifted away, the closeness began to fray. The laughs have now stopped today, no longer wanting to be on display. Once such amazing lovers, it is now gone past trying to rediscover. From the last time I held her hand, knowing none of this was ever planned.

SOULMATES NO MORE

Once were the days our love ran wild, careless, and free we always promised to be. Days turned to weeks, weeks into months yet the love we shared only grew from there. Months go by something is off, one of us stopped caring something is no longer there. Once strangers we were, lovers we turned just like a flower blooms on a summer day. Lovers we were the amazing love we shared until one drifted away. Lovers no longer, strangers again leaving one with so many unanswered questions that eat at him. No more random texts, calls have all stopped, she is now like a shadow on a lonely fall night. Soulmates once before, maybe soulmates are just a myth, a mean heartless joke only the universe gets.

LOVING ME

LOVING ME CAME SO EASY TO YOU,
EVEN WITH MY WOUNDS RUNNING
THROUGH AND THROUGH. TELLING ME
THAT YOU WOULD NEVER HURT ME.
YOU STILL WENT ON A FUCKING MURDERING SPREE.

DOING ALL THE THINGS THEY DID BEFORE,
SHAKING ME TO MY FUCKING CORE. LEAVING
ME BROKEN AND DAMAGED, CLAIMING YOU
HAD ENOUGH OF MY GODDAMN BAGGAGE. I
WILL NEVER TRUST AGAIN; MY HEART IS NOW SHACKLED
WITH CHAINS.

A PERSON OF NO WORTH

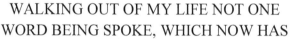

WALKING OUT OF MY LIFE NOT ONE
WORD BEING SPOKE, WHICH NOW HAS
ME WONDERING "I AM BEYOND BROKE." LOVE BEING
ONLY A WORD I ONCE HEARD, NEVER TRULY KNOWING
ANYONES WORTH. BEING UNLOVABLE LIKE A DISTANT
CURSE SET FROM LONG BEFORE OR IS IT SIMPLY NO ONE
CAN LOVE A PERSON OF NO WORTH. GIVING EVERY
OUNCE OF WHAT I BELIEVED WAS LOVE, I AM GUESSING
MY DEFINITION HAVING ME MISLEAD.

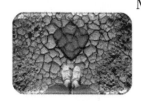

I WILL DRIFT THROUGH TIME ONLY
WISHING ONE DAY, SOMEONE WILL
LOVE A PERSON OF NO WORTH.

FORCE

WITH THE FORCE AS POWERFUL AS A DYING STAR, WITHIN A FRACTION OF A SECOND AS IT SLOWLY FADED DYING TILL NONE. THEIR TIME TOGETHER BURNT HOTTER THAN THIS SUPERNOVA, YET IT RAN ITS COURSE BUT OH THE INTENSITY IT ONCE HAD AND THAT WILL FOREVER BE WORTH THE DESTRUCTION LEFT IN ITS WAKE UP.

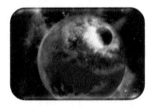

SHE CAME IN

She came in like a late summer rain, quiet and calm enchanting your soul. Smashing like a fierce ocean storm unpredictable of the damages to be told.

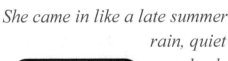

She walked out leaving destruction and death but what a beautiful sight it was to see.

THE DAY YOU LEFT

THE DAY YOU LEFT ME MY WORLD STOPPED SPINNING. MY HEART WAS RIPPED FROM MY VERY CHEST. NOW THAT 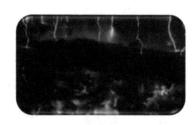 THE STORM HAS CLEARED AND THE PAIN IS SLOWLY DYING, I SIT WITH MY HEART CAREFULLY TRYING TO CUT AWAY WHAT YOU LEFT THAT DAY. I JUST COULDN'T DO IT, CUTTING AWAY ALL THE PAIN YOU LEFT ME WITH THAT DAY WOULD ALSO REMOVE ALL THE LOVE YOU  ONCE GAVE. THAT WOULD BE A DISASTER EVEN BIGGER THAN WHAT YOU NEVER MEANT TO CAUSE.

MISSING YOU THIS MUCH

 IT'S SAD WHEN YOU MISS SOMEONE THIS MUCH. GOING FROM DAILY LAUGHTER AND JOKES TO LIKE WE NEVER EVEN MET. THIS COLD EMPTY PLACE I NOW KNOW IT IS YOUR LOVE THAT IS MISSING. HOW DID I LET THIS HAPPEN, WHY DID I LET IT GET SO BAD? I WOULD AND WILL GIVE ANYTHING TO HAVE THE FEELING BACK. YOU WERE MY WORLD, MY GO TO GIRL. NOTHING WILL EVER BE THE SAME. MAYBE THAT IS MY FATE. HER PLAN FOR ME, DESTINED TO BE ALONE FOR CAUSING YOU SO MUCH PAIN. IF THAT IS MY FUTURE SO BE IT, AT LEAST I HOPE YOU WILL FIND HAPPINESS ONE DAY. IF THINGS SHOULD CHANGE AS THEY SOMETIMES DO, KNOW MY HEART WILL ALWAYS BE OPEN FOR YOU.

I'M LOST FOR WORDS

 I AM LOST FOR WORDS, THIS FEELING OF DESPAIR. NOT HAVING YOU WITH ME, NO WORDS CAN EVEN BE SPOKEN, HOW DID I LET IT GET SO BAD. YOU WERE MY WORLD, NOW YOU ARE NO LONGER THERE. REACHING FOR MY PHONE JUST MAYBE A MESSAGE IS THERE, ASKING TO TALK WONDERING IF YOU MISSED ME TOO. THAT DAY WILL NEVER COME, YOU HAVE MOVED ON, FOUND A NEW LOVE. THAT ALONE KEEPS ME UP AT NIGHT. IF GIVEN ONE MORE TRY, ONE FINAL STAND, I WOULD WISH YOU WERE BACK IN MY ARMS AT LAST. OUR LOVE GIVEN BACK;  A LESSON LEARNED. A LOVE LIKE YOURS ONLY COMES AROUND ONCE IN A LIFETIME.

COWARDLY

You left me with
no words, cowardly
having someone else
try to explain, or

maybe it was not your fault
someone's puppet you became. Leaving me
with no answers, while you sat back and
watched me spiral. In my heart I know that is
not you, controlled by someone honey the signs
were always there. I slowly pick up your
destruction, carefully examining every
piece. I will probably never be as I
was before; trusting is no longer
there. I do not hate you, never in
my life will I use that word. In my
heart I know one day, the situation be
reversed, and you will finally feel this pain.
As you are slowly cleaning up in his wake, that
emptiness will hit you at last. Knowing now that
is how you left me that day, I do not wish this
pain upon you, but Karma repays the exact same
way. Maybe that day will come when you are
able to see, the man you claimed you loved
deserved better than what you were told to say,
but being controlled wasn't part of your plan.
My love for you will never disappear, I made
you a promises I would always be near.

BRAVE FACE

 I have put on my brave face; I still want to believe you would not want me sad. Pushing you and our memories to the back of my mind, knowing dormant they will not stay. Like a summer storm blowing in, an image of you surfaced. Wave of emotions slamming into my soul, like sheets of that rain, tears run down my face, no this is not supposed to happen. I am replaying that day over in my head, how could you of all people do it so freely. With that same storm it changed so quickly how is this the same girl who absolutely loved me. I was your always to my forever. storm subsided tears slowly drifting, just as fast as this mid-summer storm, our love disappeared with it. A smile slowly forming, like the sun emerging from once gray clouds. I will be good just as long as I know that somewhere out there you are happy and loved.

TWO STRANGERS

Just like that two strangers finally meet, their attraction for each other was not discreet. With the perfection of the moment, neither one had words that could be spoke. Two perfect strangers now lovers these days, yet only one can see as this love slowly decays. Their flame that once burnt bright as the sun, slowly dies down and flickers until none. Just like that these two lovers before, are now two perfect strangers and lovers no more.

IF I WOULD HAVE KNOWN

If I would have known then what I know in the now, all the love I gave to you I would disallow. The moments I looked into your eyes; I should have clearly seen my own demise. I gave you all the broken pieces of my heart, knowing it was broken you still managed to rip it apart. Strangers we eventually became, you still in denial throwing me all the blame. Even though you are gone your presence is still here, you do not want me, yet you will not disappear. Everything about you still haunts me to this day, you enjoy having me your victim and prey. Removing you out of my life completely, the torturous and evil ways you can no longer treat me.

HIS CONTROL

He says he loves me; he says
that he cares, yet at
the same time he does not
even want me there. I have
learned to deal with that,
kinda had to get used to
it; screams at me I will never do
better than whispers that he does it
because he cares. Taken full control, it is
kinda nice having such a hold, I am a whore
for making myself look nice, even after crying
out I only did it for him. Have a
tight schedule to keep, I have to
obliged to his demands,
blackeyes do not go with my sun
kissed tan. Staying cause, I see
the good, he will go back to what he
used to be. Deaf and blind I have become, a
hollow shell I am today giving up completely
numb. Today that shell finally cracked, fuck his
feelings I am done with that. No more mind
games, no more control, able to do like before. I
have done better despite what he screamed, now
he sits and cry's and wonders how another man
has made me smile, with only such words he
never learned. A princess today no longer a
slave, a man who loves me for me. Never in my
wildest dreams could I have seen someone love
such a damaged girl like me.

FUCKING GAMES

Loving me from the start was nothing more than a stage in your act. Telling me what I wanted to hear so you felt better about your roll in this part. Feeding into this fake love affair while I sat like a fool while you had your own

fucked up affair. Games you played with my head knowing goddamn well I was already fucked up there. Your game is up the proof is out, now karma is about to play her part. Comes around goes around and without a doubt the best part of this play has yet to play out. Feelings now destroyed crushed beyond repair but do not think this is all of this tangled love affair. Placing the blame solely on me as I sat and watched in complete disbelief. My soul now crushed my heart beyond shattered as you stand over tall no remorse, shame not even there. Just like the evil storms from my not too distant past, you are now the worst of them a category that will forever last. Empty inside wondering how I was to blame; I was not the one cheating and being played like a child's game. Your plan is done the prize is ready to be claimed another soul to now call only yours.

YOU CAME IN

You came without warning entering my life, like the coming of a storm
when it first blows in. Silent and calm as beautiful as the setting sun,
your violent force crashing down that day, once calm now a raging
storm you became. Your voice echoing like thunder, your hail of hate
ripping the heart you finally fixed.
Devastation and destruction left in
your wake, leaving me lost and
deserted completely numb hollow
once again.

FINISH OFF HIS LOVE

Finally finishing off the last of his love,
bitter at first but now words will flow like
an F5. Blowing through leaving tears
rushing, flooding her heart drowning her
once greatest and now last of her love.

YOUR DAY

YOUR DAY IS HAPPENING IT HURTS THAT YOUR DAILY PATTERNS ARE ETCHED FOREVER IN MY HEAD. SITTING HERE THINKING OF TIMES WE HAD, I WONDER IF YOU ARE DOING OK. AS OUR DAY SLOWLY COMES TO A CLOSE, MY TORTUROUS NIGHT SOON WILL BEGIN. LAYING IN MY DARK ROOM HAUNTED BY MY MEMORIES OF YOU. AS YOU LAY DOWN FOR BED DO I EVEN CROSS YOUR MIND. DO YOU EVER SIT AND WONDER THE SAME AS I DO FOR YOU? IF I CROSSED YOUR MIND AS MUCH AS YOU DO MINE, REACHING OUT JUST TO SAY HI WOULD COME AS EASY AS YOU ARE CROSSING MY MIND.

ANOTHER CHAPTER

*TODAY ANOTHER CHAPTER
I HAVE CLOSED, WITH IT
BEING THE BEST YET. FROM
THE MOMENT I FIRST SAW
HER EYES, WHAT CHANCE DID
I EVER REALLY HAVE.
ALTHOUGH A BRIEF TIME WE
HAD, BUILDING SUCH GRAND
MEMORIES. MEMORIES OF LOVE, SOME MEMORIES
SAD, TO THE GRANDEST OF THEM ALL, NOW THAT
ONE IS MINE TO KEEP. TIME CHANGES PEOPLE,
DISTANCE DID NOT HELP. REGRETTING NOT
ONE MINUTE UP UNTIL THE END,
THINGS GOT SOUR I WILL
TAKE ALL THE BLAME.
PLEASE KNOW TILL YOUR
FINAL DAY, MY LOVE FOR
YOU IGNITED A FLAME, A
FLAME THAT KEPT MY DEMONS
AT BAY. TIME SHALL PASS MORE
CHAPTERS WILL TURN, BUT ALWAYS
KNOW IN MY BOOK OF LIFE, OUR CHAPTER WILL BE
THE GREATEST ADVENTURE I EVER TOOK.*

UNDELIVERABLE

BABY TODAY WAS AN AMAZING
DAY; EVERYTHING WENT RIGHT I DID NOT HAVE
A PANIC ATTACK. I WAS ABLE TO GO INTO THE
STORE WITHOUT YOUR LUCKY CHARM, I NEEDED
TO TRY I HOPE YOU KNOW THAT. WORK WAS
PERFECT I
FINALLY GOT
THAT
PROMOTION MY
TRIP TO SEE YOU

THAT MUCH CLOSER. REST OF MY DAY DRAGGED
ON, BOARD MEETING USELESS STUFF. FINALLY
GETTING HOME YOU KNOW HOW I HATE THAT
DRIVE. I REACH FOR MY PHONE EXCITED TO TELL
YOU ABOUT MY DAY, THEN IT SLOWLY HIT ME I
CANNOT TELL YOU, NO LONGER TOGETHER THAT
END A MONTH BEFORE.

INSIDE A NARCISSISTIC MIND

LYING TO YOU ABOUT EVERYTHING. SAYING I LOVE MYSELF ALL THE WHILE HATING MYSELF. IT IS NOT HOW I WANT IT TO BE, CHOOSING THIS SO EARLY IN LIFE. BEING SO SENSITIVE; FEELING TOO MUCH, MADE TO FEEL I WAS NEVER ENOUGH. BEING HURT AND ABUSED, STRONG AND COLD NOW WHAT OTHER CHOICE DID I HAVE. BEING STRONG WAS ALL I HAD; NOT ALLOWING MYSELF TO FEEL, CUTTING LOVE OFF WAS IT ALL THAT BAD. I NOW WEAR THIS MASK, THIS MASK OF LIES. KEEPING ME FROM FEELING INSIDE. I WILL COME OFF AS NICE, GET COMFORTABLE CAUSE FUCK YOUR FEELINGS SO WHAT IF YOU ARE HURT. IF ONLY YOU COULD SEE AND FEEL FROM INSIDE A NARCISSISTIC MIND.

CONFUSION

HAVING GIVEN ME THE WORLD, YOU SHOWED ME A SIDE UNLIKE ANY OTHER. GIVING ME A LOVE, I'VE NEVER FELT, NEVER TRULY KNOWING MY OWN WORTH. PICKING ME UP WHEN I WAS LOW, BUILDING ME BACK UP STRONG WE ONCE STOOD. PROMISES ME THINGS WOULD NEVER

CHANGE, HITTING ME LIKE A BRICK WHEN ALL YOUR CHANGES CAME. NO LONGER MY GO TO GIRL, LEAVING ME FLOATING IN THIS NEW AND UNKNOWN WORLD. NO EXPLANATION FOR LEAVING, NOT A WORD TO BE SPOKEN. LOVING SOMEONE SO MUCH AS I DID WITH YOU, HOW COULD SOMEONE BEGIN TO HATE YOU.

MY UNKNOWN

YOU HAVE BEEN RIPPED AND TORN APART, BEATEN DOWN SHATTERED BEYOND REPAIR. CLAIMED YOU WERE LOVED, TOLD YOU MATTERED. DEPRESSION NOW  HAUNTS YOU, CONSUMES YOUR ENTIRE BEING. WHEN YOU FEEL LOST AND HAVE GIVEN UP ON HOPE, THAT IS WHEN YOU STAND ON YOUR OWN AND STRONG. NO ONE WAS THERE WHEN YOU FELL, NO ONE CAUGHT YOU AT THE BOTTOM.  STANDING ON YOUR OWN TWO FEET; YOU DO NOT NEED ANYONE. IN THE WAKE OF YOUR DEVASTATION, ON THE EDGE OF YOUR UNKNOWN STANDING TALL CAUSE THAT IS ALL YOU KNOW. FAILURE IS NOT AN OPTION, NOR WILL YOU STAND FOR IT ANYMORE.

DARK DAYS

WALKING THROUGH LIFE
ONLY THINKING FOR ONE,
NO CARES FOR OTHERS
ABSOLUTELY NONE.
SELFISH AND HEARTLESS HE
WAS PERCEIVED YET HAVING THEM ALL DECEIVED.
SOCIETY HAS MOLDED HIS BLACKENED SOUL, WITH
EVERYDAY SINKING SLOWER INTO ITS BLACKHOLE.
WE HAVE NO ONE TO BLAME, WE ALL HOLD THAT
SHAME. SO MUCH ANGER AND
HATE, THIS WAS NOT THE PLAN
LAID DOWN BY FATE. NEVER ANY
THOUGHTS REMORSE OR
REGRET, THEY HAVE NOT SEEN
THE WORST OF IT YET. DARK
DAYS WILL COME, A LOT SOONER
FOR SOME. COMPASSION AND
LOVE WILL BE LIKE A LANGUAGE
UNKNOWN, ALL THEIR HATE AND DESTRUCTION
WILL FINALLY BE SHOWN. THEIR FATE FOREVER
SEALED, ALL IN PART TO THEIR COMPASSION
UNHEALED.

CATACLYSM

LIKE A SHADOW OF DOUBT CURSED WITH
UNCERTAINTY, HIS HEART AND SOUL BRACE SO
FEARFULLY.
ALWAYS FILLED WITH
OPTIMISM, WHILE BEING
SURROUNDED BY
CATACLYSM. DOWN THIS
ROAD WITH THE PAIN MANY
TIMES BEFORE, LIKE A MASOCHIST HE IS ALWAYS
THERE FOR MORE. EMPTINESS IS ALL HE KNOWS,
ALWAYS LEAVING HIS HEART EXPOSED.
LEARNING TO ENTER LOVE KNOWING ONLY TIME
WILL TELL, HIS NEWFOUND POWER NEVER TO
DWELL. ALONE AGAIN YOU WOULD HAVE
THOUGHT MAYBE THIS TIME THINGS WOULD
HAVE CHANGED; HE IS ACCEPTED HIS FATE A
LOVELESS LIFE WILL FOREVER REMAIN

LOST LOVE

Once so close, once my forever. Those were the days our love was so connected. Lovers no more, today it seems like her chore. Slowly our fire flickers, all I have left are her pictures. Lovers yesterday; strangers we have become, maybe my love was never good enough. All that I want is for her happiness, even if I am not the man, she spends the rest of her life with.

GHOST

Ghosts of my past haunt me daily it is almost like walking on glass. Tormenting and prying at my armor, clawing, and trying harder. My battle I thought I had already won; my demons now scream they are far from done. Standing tall again raising my sword, I do not wish to become their object of scorn. Battling my dark entities, knowing all my possibilities. Slaying down my monsters, never again will they return forever now slaughtered.

MY FINAL ACT

THIS WILL BE MY FINAL ACT, NO
MORE DWELLING OR LOOKING
BACK. ALL THE HURT I FEEL TODAY,
WILL BE NO MORE EVER AGAIN. CLOSING THIS
CHAPTER ON THIS DISASTER, PAIN NO MORE NOT
EVEN LAUGHTER. MY LIFE WAS GOOD, IT WAS
GRAND EVEN BATTLING THROUGH HELL AND BACK.
I HAVE NO REGRETS, NO LEFTOVER HEARTACHE.
THIS WAS DESTINED TO BE MY FINAL ACT, NO MORE
HIDING NO MORE RUNNING. THE HIDING BEHIND
HUMOR AND SMILES, FINALLY FREE OF THAT FAKE
PERSONA. YOU SET ME FREE YOU SHOULD BE
PROUD, NOW YOU GET TO LIVE YOUR LIFE WITHOUT
CARE. PLEASE KNOW I LOVED YOU TO THE END, BUT
WHAT YOU DID SEALED MY FATE. DRY YOUR TEARS
WIPE THOSE EYES, STARS   CANNOT
SHINE ON RAINY
NIGHTS. BE THAT HAPPY
ONCE FREE, EVER SO
LOVING GIRL I GOT TO
MEET. MY PAIN IS
GONE, YOU WILL NO
LONGER CARE NOT EVEN A
WHISPER OF MY NAME WILL BREAK
YOUR AIR. MY TIME IS UP FOR ME TO GO, PLEASE
ALWAYS KNOW YOU ARE MY LAST TRUE LOVE NO
MORE SHALL EVER BE.

YOUR HAPPINESS

NEVER REALLY KNOWING
THIS DAY WOULD COME,
ALWAYS THOUGHT OUR
CALLS WOULD HAPPEN.

TAKING FOR GRANTED ALL THAT I HAD, IS WHAT
YOU CLAIMED I DID AND NO LONGER CARED. THE
FACT IS MY LOVE FOR YOU WAS STRONGER THAN
EVER, I CARED FOR YOU EVEN WHEN YOU ARE NOT
THERE. MAYBE THE DAY WILL COME YOU FIND YOUR
WAY HOME, AND EVERYTHING WILL GO BACK TO
THE WAY IT WAS BEFORE. IF THAT SHOULD NEVER
HAPPEN, AND YEARS PASS US BY AS LONG AS YOU

FIND HAPPINESS THAT IS ALL THAT I
CARE. YOU DESERVE THE HAPPINESS
YOU READ ABOUT IN BOOKS, ONLY
THIS WILL NOT BE A FAIRYTALE FOR
YOU, IT WILL BE YOUR DREAM COME
TRUE.

HER FINAL BATTLE

THIS DARK ENTITY CONSUMES HER AGAIN. HER BEST FRIEND NOW KNOWN AS DEPRESSION, LEAVING HER LIFE AND EXISTENCE ALL IN QUESTION. GIVING UP RELIEF AND PEACE SOUNDS SO BITTERSWEET. FINALLY TIRED OF THE PAIN, REALIZING THERE

IS NOTHING MORE TO GAIN. SHE SEES NO END TO THIS DARK AND HAUNTING MONSTER, WITHIN HERSELF THE STRENGTH SHE MUST CONJURE. STANDING TALL AGAINST THIS DEMON, AS THE PAIN ONLY DEEPENS. NO ONE CAN SAVE HER NOW. SHE IS TIRED OF LETTING PEOPLE DOWN. THIS WILL BE HER ULTIMATE BATTLE, THE HOLD HER MONSTER ONCE HAD; THE TIME HAS COME TO BREAK ITS SHACKLES.

ETERNAL BUTTERFLIES

They say every single person has that one true love, so pure and true being forged with the fabric of time. As with every masterpiece fate had to make sure their forge would withstand. The universe having a hand in evaluating the strength making sure it is ironclad. Now not to mislead with this masterpiece, this too has been written into their original plan. Now these lost and drifting souls will collide, but their bond was never meant to hold. Damaged and wounded they both are, forming a temporary bond lessons were being given. Both needing to know the absolute power of self- love so they may return to their one true love. Each of these once tattered and damaged souls now in their cocoon slowly growing into what they were always destined to be for their forever one.

Sadness, grief, heartache and even despair as sad as it seems will be there greatest trials and tribulations. Every living thing needs to be prepared and molded in life for when the time is right this unbreakable bond forged before time began can finally break free from its cocoon so the destined to be soulmates will finally and fully experience the magical feeling when they finally meet they will have the full effects of the "butterflies."

THANK YOU

Thank you, you made me a better person than I once was. You showed me a side of life I will never forget. You gave me a feeling I have never felt before. I will cherish all our

memories. Yes, I am sad, yes, I am hurt, confused and sometimes angry but I am getting better. If your happiness is the result of this, then I am happy you are happy. You truly showed me a side of life I never knew existed so thank you. I will always love you and I will always be here for you no matter what, not even the months that should pass even years too, my love for you will never fade or go away.

GREW UP TOO FAST

Eyes so bright and brown in color, witnessed hell by the hand of his mother. Scared and alone he did not know what to believe, he grew up too fast he ran wild and free. Not knowing what to do or who to be, one wintry night someone extended a hand; he never knew this person was his #1 fan. Sitting back watching waiting with love to give, encouraging words, food, and a safe place to live. They built back a bond that was once broken, a bond they now hold dear like a golden token. With words of wisdom this father would set back and see, his son

grows into the warrior he always knew he would be. The little boy with eyes brown in color, now a man with strength like no other. He slays his demons, wins war after war. With his father at his side. He keeps coming back for more. His father watches on with pride. Smiling at every stride. Witnessing his son become a man and he will forever be his #1 fan.

CHAPTERS

As I sit back and watch as he puts his life on paper I watch as his eyes shift from now to later. He is going over memories some good some bad. He is thinking about the crazy life he has had. He is loved without bounds, been hurt time and time again. He has slayed demons some die going against. He has taken his pain and struggle and is using it for good. He has shown me a love I never thought someone could. He has taken my heart; he has it

with him. I hope in this story of his life, my name will be written. Not in the beginning, or the middle but at the very end. I sit back and watch him write his life with a pen. Loving this man is all I know. I hope just like the chapters, our love will continue to grow.

I'M DOING GOOD

Lately people have been asking "how are you doing" I simply reply "I am doing good." However, the truth of the matter is I am not fine, not even close. How does one even begin to describe how they feel when they do not even know how they feel? Almost like I am slowly drowning without a drop of water. Like a splinter left to fester through the skin. Like a cancer slowly eating away your insides, but its only just the mention of a word, place, or name. Walls start closing in, even with unlimited space around. So how does one begin to describe what we are feeling inside, we simply slide on our new favorite fake smile and reply "I'm doing good." Living this way almost every day, haunting you like a dark murderous entity. Why would one even begin to describe such pain and horror, when you alone are barely holding by a thread. No one should ever have to know such torture and pain that would slowly drive them absolutely insane. appetite is for the soul that is almost dead. The tight aching burn in your chest when

THE LOVE THEY WRITE ABOUT

She could only dream of a love that you would read about. Being loved by her one and only was so far from being reality. That kiss that would take her breath away, a touch that would give her goosebumps. Her one true prince would soon be found in a place she would have never guessed. With such a simple touch, the only touch she had dreamed of. Not having much, not able to offer a lot; still giving her the broken pieces of his heart. Never feeling she was good enough, her prince showed her exactly what she was worth. Such a simple smile, eyes that could light up the night. There was nothing he would have changed, nothing he would want to change. She was amazing in every aspect of her being. They were designed to be together, it had always been written; it was fates grand design

SHE LOVES WITH NO REGARD

She loves with no regard, for her own heart as it lays dormant in a box. Mesmerizing and captivating eyes, yet you can clearly see the pain and suffering she has hidden inside. Always thinking of others, always saying there is no time for selfish little girls. Coming to terms that she will never be of worth, settling for what comes her way. Grief and despair, she swims in like the ocean's waves; all the while she dreams of her day.

Butterfly kisses, cosmic storms in his eyes; feeling his stare her soul now ignites. New feelings surge through her soul, with one single kiss melting and molding two hearts into one. Finding what she is only felt in dreams, his single touch released its once evil clutch. Universes in her eyes, despair vanished that day; cosmic storms burning so bright. This loveless goddess once disallowed such an amazing new clutch.

WALLS GO UP

As I sit here with tears streaming down my face, knowing deep down a life lesson I just learned and learned the hard way this will take years to heal. Maybe I do not know all there is about love. A woman knows her worth do not ever forget that. When she slowly starts to feel he no longer cares, this switch is flipped not on purpose either. She slowly starts to feel unwanted no longer loved the same. She will distance herself and not to be mean, she is doing that only to protect her heart. She knows that time will come when he will no longer be there, nothing but an amazing love they once shared. When that finally happens, there is no turning back, her heart is in protection mode and no key or hidden switch will change any of that. If you have 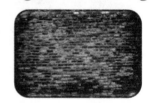 *an amazing girl who loves you with all her heart and would go to war for you just to keep you out of harm's way. If you have a girl that looks at you like you are the greatest thing alive. If you have a girl that never stops cheering for you to do better because she sees something in you that no one else did. Do not lose sight of that amazing incredible girl because speaking from experience once her little switch gets flipped nothing and no one can change any of that. Her heart now in charge, will protect her at any cost. When that day comes, that will be the day you will have lost the most amazing girl to have ever loved you.*

SUNKEN TREASURE

*Deep in my soul, buried
beneath my heart. Like a
sunken treasure, lost in an
ocean of weather. Feelings inside I hide so*

*well, if only it were so
easy instead, I chose
to dwell. Maybe one
day she will dig up
this chest, the day she
will no longer guess. Unearthing these
feelings once buried so deep, awaking my
soul which was once asleep. Feeling her
tender touch, she will finally release this
clutch. Her love for me unlike any I have
seen, she will make me her king, she will
forever be my queen.*

HIS LOVE NO LONGER

HIS LOVE FOR ME NO LONGER THERE, THE UNFAMILIAR PRESENCE FROM HIS GLARE. ONCE HOLDING ME EVER SO TIGHT, DECLARING HIS LOVE HE WOULD NOT GO DOWN WITHOUT A FIGHT. THOSE DAYS ARE GONE, THE LOVE WE ONCE HAD IS NOW FOREGONE. STRANGERS THESE DAYS, SO HARD TO BELIEVE THIS FIRE INSIDE HIM ONCE WAS A BLAZE. TIME WILL HEAL THIS PAIN, MAYBE MINE WILL TOO; EVEN AFTER HE SPIT HIS DISDAIN.

But you **promised**! :(

HER PICTURE

*I saw your picture today, your
vibrant yet dangerous smile
caught my eye. The soft
glow coming from those
eyes drew me in like a
speechless spell, casting
itself upon my soul. Dark
and sad, yet alive and playful.
Looking closer, you have been hurt
too many times, not understanding how a
man could not love such a dark and
mysterious girl like you. If only I knew you
better, you would see you are the mysterious
dark girl that walks in my dreams.*

KALEIDOSCOPE HEART

*Loving someone who does not love
you, wanting someone that does
not want you. Rips and shatters
her heart, slowly tearing the soul
apart. Never understood, never a
reason why; it is so hard to shut
that door saying goodbye. Toying with her
emotions, destructive like the waves of an
ocean. Her heart is like a kaleidoscope,
colors change from despair to hope.*

YET I STILL FELL IN LOVE

Yet I still fell in love with you knowing the
violent storm

you brought with. Now I am
here picking up the pieces of

my once again shattered heart,
but my God what a

beautiful, sexual catastrophe it
was shaking me down to

my very core. Only if you
were like other storms, I would

brace for your devastation; patiently waiting for
your

return.

BEAUTIFUL GIRL

BEAUTIFUL
GIRL WITH
SUNLIGHT IN HER
HAIR. THE ONE WITH
THE SMILE THAT ALWAYS MADE
THE PAIN GO AWAY. THE ONE WITH
THE EYES, THE EYES FULL OF STARS
AND GALAXIES THAT NO MATTER
HOW FAR YOU WERE LOST THEY
WERE ALWAYS THERE TO GUIDE
YOUR WAY BACK.
BEAUTIFUL GIRL I SEE
YOU TODAY WITH THAT
STORM IN YOUR HEAD,
THAT AMAZING SMILE
GONE, OH, BEAUTIFUL
GIRL I FEEL YOUR PAIN.
THOSE EYES ARE NOW FULL
OF COSMIC DUST OF THE
SUDDEN COLLAPSE OF THOSE
ONCE BRILLIANT AND STUNNING
STARS. I HOPE THAT ONE DAY YOU
WILL NOT NEED WHAT YOU THINK
SOUNDS GOOD AT THE TIME, NO
BEAUTIFUL GIRL YOU DESERVE SO
MUCH MORE, THOSE GALAXIES
WILL ALWAYS FIND A WAY TO
SHINE.

DOESN'T EVEN KNOW I'M THERE

There is something about you, those eyes filled with such loneliness yet shows all the love you would give to the right man that understood your darkness. A smile that could light my darkest nights. Oh, if fate could rewrite history the world would fall in love seeing all the love that we share. Showering each other with love unheard of, our dark lonely worlds would finally be one. But it does not work like that, fate had other plans unfortunately. You hardly even know me or that I am even there, but I can still have all this in my dreams.

MYSTERY GIRL

Who was this mystery girl, that smile gently pulling my soul towards her? Was this what so many have spoken of, a whole new feeling this flutter in my chest. As how the universe works pulling all matter together, our souls spinning and twirling form so complete.

Captivating smile mesmerizing eyes, as she walked my way what chance did I ever have. Fate does not always work in our favor, with a simple hi as she passed by. Like the universe particles and fragments pass right through, the cosmic pull as the one we just passed through

BACK AT IT AGAIN

Look at that, we are back at it yet again. I know you have been hurt; love you have been denied. They punched and bruised your soul, your heart tattered and left dull. Babygirl I need you to know, I am not like them I see you still have your doubts though. Beautiful broken girl, I want to show you a whole new world. Let me mend those pieces, trust me I know you have heard these speeches. My love for you I will show, until every broken part begins to glow. I promise you; you will see, your once trapped soul I will finally set free

PAST TRAUMA

Past trauma severe mental damage, wondering if love will ever find me with all this baggage. Always worried never being understanding, from the start, liars and cheaters already branding. Maybe one day this trauma will deplete, when my heart once again is finally complete.

FRAGILE

Fragile and broken pieces, never able to mend or bind; swearing off love now fully blind. No longer wanting his touch, slowly she became numb; always dealing with the same outcome. Darkness now consumes, at long last she was knowing love; falling for the moon above. Moon light in her eyes, star dust in her hair; she finally has met her new love affair.

HER WOUNDS

Wounds so deep, scars on her heart; having her soul violently ripped apart. Pieces left broken damaged beyond repair, the feeling of love now in despair. A simple hello, seeing through her demise; the real girl he saw deep in those eyes. Pieces now left weathered and tattered, picking them up despite being shattered. Slowly putting them back together, wanting her to know her love will forever be treasured.

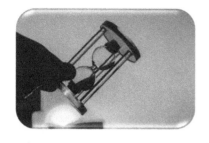

SO MANY BEFORE

So many before her left him broken and scared. His heart always being ripped and torn apart. His lonely world covered with darkness, to him it was beautiful and seemed so harmless. Never really needing or wanting it to be seen, shrouded by clouds of mystery her beauty was not unseen.

She entered his soul peeling back layers of black. Slowly revealing all the years of torment and pain, wondering why or how this man stayed so sane.

HIS DARKNESS

His darkness was his, which he

wore like a

badge,

others saw it as a cadge. He perceived it as a greatness, living now complete and painless.

THE SLEEPING BEAST

AS I SLOWLY OPEN MY EYES, DREADING THE LIGHT FROM THE SUN. TODAY WILL BE SO MUCH BETTER WAIT AND SEE IF I DO NOT WAKE THE SLEEPING BEAST. TIP TOE EVER SO SLOW WE KNOW WHAT WILL HAPPEN IF HE HEARS THE SLIGHTEST NOISE. HOW DID THIS COME TO BE REMEMBERING BACK WHEN I WAS SO FREE? NOW LIVING WITHIN THESE WALLS, HE IS MY OWN PERSONAL HELL. MAYBE ONE DAY HE WILL CHANGE JUST MAYBE HE WILL BE THE MAN HE USED TO BE.

MONSTERS AND SHADOWS

MONSTERS AND WILD, TORMENT AND WHILE THEY SMILE. THE MIND, BINDING, INTERTWINING. NOW CONSUMES, THE PIERCING THE SOUL HARPOONS.

SHADOWS RUN PAIN ALL THE DESTROYING AND DARKNESS DEMONS SHARP AS

I HATE NIGHTS LIKE THIS

*I HATE NIGHTS WHERE I FEEL SO
HOLLOW INSIDE, I FEEL SO
DAMN EMPTY AND OUT OF
PLACE. I HATE THE NIGHTS
WHERE MY MIND WANDERS TO
THE UNKNOWN AND ALL
I RETURN WITH IS
SADNESS. I HATE
COUNTING THE TEARS
THAT RUSH DOWN MY
CHEEKS AND COLLECT
UPON MY PILLOW. I
HATE THAT THE ONLY
THING AT NIGHT TO COMFORT
ME IS MY LONELINESS AND THE
ONLY THING I FEEL
SURROUNDING ME IS DARKNESS.*

A NEW DAY

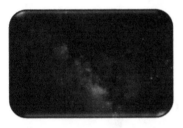

DARKNESS CONSUMES MY MIND, DEMONS SWIMMING INTERTWINED. SO MANY PAST MISTAKES, THIS DAY THERE IS FAR MORE AT STAKE. CRAWLING AND CLIMBING THIS PERSONAL HELL, THIS ISSUE I NO LONGER WILL DWELL. THIS BATTLE I FINALLY WON, A NEW DAY HAS NOW BEGUN

MY MONSTER

THE MONSTER ONCE BURIED IN THE DEPTH, THE ONE I HAD ONCE THOUGHT PUT TO DEATH. DEMONS SCRATCH AND CLAW

WANTING AN UP RISE, CHAOS, AND DESTRUCTION IN THEIR EYES. THIS DAY FULLY ARMED, STANDING UPRIGHT I AM LEFT UNHARMED.

ABANDONED

*Our biggest downfall is making
problems where there are not
any. Pushing people away
before they can leave us. Being*
abandoned again is not something we want.

MY ARMOR

 *Monsters clawing and
scratching like a
cancer slowly
attacking. Draining
my essence, making
their presence known. Fighting a never-
ending battle, attacking like a jackal. My
armor this time full and restored to its prime.
These monsters of mine, this time they will
remain confined.*

DANCING DEMONS

Darkness you cannot see, demons all around like scree.  Draining within myself, my soul dying in itself. Demons dancing with glee, running rampant so carefree. Control was lost, that fine line has been crossed. Taking back control, my soul will again be absolute and whole.

INSANE

 Once was I sane, I now only have her to blame. No longer am I in pain, touching my heart making love to my soul, forever will I be insane.

HE SAW/SHE SAW

She saw him, he saw her, she saw her forever, he never thought she would be his end.

He saw her, she saw him. He saw his forever, she never thought he would be her end.

KISSING HER LIPS

KISSING HER LIPS, GENTLE AND SOFT; SHE FINALLY LET GO ALL THAT HURT WAS LOST. BROKEN PIECES ONCE BEFORE, SWIMMING IN HER OCEAN OF PAIN ALWAYS SO GUARDED, HER HEART WILL NEVER BE GIVEN AGAIN. THOUGHTS THROWN OUT THE WINDOW, RULES WILL NOW BE BROKEN. JUST FROM HIS TOUCH, HER SOUL AT LAST HAD FINALLY BEEN AWOKE.

HER ONCE PAINFUL CLUTCH

Darkness all around; moonlight in her eyes, it was at night she felt so alive. Galaxy kisses, cosmic stares, her eyes just like a solar flare. Universes in her soul; yet she was never quite there, all the pain she carried other people did not even care. She craved a touch, a soft gentle touch, the one that will release this painful clutch.

HER OCEAN

And I would love to swim in your ocean and inhale all your thoughts. Go inside your mind to see all that is so divine. Wrap you in my arms to feel your beating heart. A whole new world you would see no more darkness guaranteed.

SEEING HOW

Seeing how you moved on before our love was even done. A love once that  *made us feel so complete and pure, yet you threw it aside like a broken child's toy. You must have got bored or did not get your way. No explanation or reasoning just hateful names you say today, when once you called me your perfectly perfect*

MONSTERS

Monsters so violate and deep, inside my soul I try to keep. Tied up and shackled ever so tight, keeping them at bay is a constant fight. Touching caressing my soul, maybe one day will keep me whole.

PUREST OF LOVE

Having someone fall in love with you and see past your physical appearance and learns to dance better than your demons is a someone who will touch your soul leaving those demons breathless.

MY MOST FAVORITE BOOK

If she were a book, she would be my most favorite book yet. Having read front to back cover,  *paying special attention to the parts only I could get. Just like her soul, the spine would be untold of. Perfect in every aspect of the word, pages never bent or torn. Marveling at all her adventures, getting excited even when I know what is already there. Taking her in my hands so gentle, like a new*

bloomed flower in a wild spring meadow. The spark of this newfound book, unlike any other pages that have been mistook. Fully understanding why her world was so dark, never could anyone else grasp such pain. Reading her like a book, she would be my most favorite of books. Never wanting to put her down, with so many questions left unsaid.

THE REGRET

One day down the road you're going to be in the middle of your daily chores or even late one night as you lay in bed and this wave of emotions is going to hit you like a fierce storm that comes out of nowhere. You may cry, you may get depressed, you may even want to make a call because you will finally have realized how badly you treated me and the hurtful things you said and did. You will see everything I did for you for was out of pure love. You will miss all those times I would check on you, those simple little texts telling you how beautiful you look that day even without seeing you. All of that will consume you and take over your mind, until you finally try to reach to me. When someone picks up the phone you hear a woman's voice and asking for me, she introduced herself as my wife. Then and only then will you finally feel all the pain and hurt I felt that unforgettable day

UNCERTAIN TIMES

Meeting at uncertain times, gravity pulling everything in line. They say everything happens for a reason, was the reason approaching. Mesmerizing eyes have, stunning heart on her smile immediately desperation and clear. Another one what chance did I beauty wearing her sleeve. Captivating my clouds of uncertainly began to of fates plans written

in the book of my so-called life. Her voice now silencing my demon's, as they sat intrigued by the music that she speaks. Compassion and genuine care was she truly sent to me in my time of despair.

THEN SHE

Having only read of a love so pure. Touching all his flaws that have been stitched together with broken promises. Seeing such unspeakable damage wondering how someone could pass over this rare treasure. His demons now silenced, the torment finally at bay. Never knowing such a voice finally calming his misery and pain. Holding him whispering softly "My love, you are now loved and forever protected. Tears falling down his cheeks, knowing that someone finally truly means it.

RARE MASTERPIECE

She is not too much to handle, you just do not know how to appreciate a rare book. Fragile pages aged from mishandling, let them flow without care. Reading all words and paragraphs, if you really listen and pay attention, she will tell you all you need to know. Her story will make you laugh, even make you cry, some chapters leaving you wondering why no one knew just how to manage such a rare treasure. Captivating and stunning the pages turn, her words you fully understand. How no one could ever appreciate such a beautiful story, all the words, phrases have never been so clear. She is an unfinished book of wonder, and with all the love I can offer this rare masterpiece I truly hope I am in her final chapters.

WALLS SO HIGH

SOMEONE AMAZING ASKED ME THE OTHER DAY, BABY WHY ARE YOUR WALLS SO HIGH. WHAT IF I WANTED TO GET IN AND SHOW YOU WHAT LOVE TRULY IS? I DID NOT KNOW WHAT TO SAY, HAVE I REALLY BUILT MY WALLS SO HIGH THAT NOTHING AND NO ONE WILL EVER GET IT. WHAT IF THIS BLUE-EYED GIRL GENUINELY WANTED TO SHOW ME WHAT A REAL LOVE FELT LIKE. THE

DEMONS INSIDE BEGAN TO PROTEST WHILE THE ANGELS ALL GATHERED AROUND INSTEAD WHISPERING "WHAT IS LOVE IF YOU NEVER TAKE THAT LEAP."

THAT FEELING

DO YOU KNOW THAT
FEELING YOU GET WHEN
YOU SEE THAT ONE PERSON
YOU KNOW YOU ARE
DESTINED TO BE WITH, THAT
ONE PERSON WHO WAS THE
ONLY ONE TO HAVE EVER
GIVEN YOU BUTTERFLIES, THE
ONLY PERSON WHO HE WOULD
GIVE HIS LIFE FOR SO HE
COULD HAVE JUST FIVE MORE
MINUTES WITH YOU AS HIS
GIRL OR BEING
AROUND THAT
PERSON THAT YOU
ABSOLUTELY LOVE
SO MUCH IT
LITERALLY HURTS.
WELL THAT IS EXACTLY WHAT
I GO THROUGH EVERY TIME
YOU ARE NEAR ME AND THE
THING THAT HURTS THE MOST
IS KNOWING THAT THERE IS
NO POSSIBLE WAY THE TWO
OF US CAN OR EVER WILL BE
TOGETHER

THE POSSIBILITIES

*Is it possible to make love to
you with only words?
Pinning you down with
every passing phrase.
Having you feel every
comma and question mark.
These sentences slowly make you shake.
Hearing you moan when you turn the page.
Satisfied now my words are part of your
body now.*

WORDS OF DESIRE

*I want to make love to you, not
normal love. I want to kiss you
with my words, tugging at your hair with my
inner thoughts. Making you gasp for air as
you read what I write. Finally stripping you
of your clothes, but not with my hands,
passionately making love with words of love,
leaving her poetically satisfied.*

WORDS OF PASSIOIN

As her body hit the bed, hair matted and sweaty across her face. Body left trembling yearning for more, wondering how someone could ever make love, passionate deep love with only words. As he read more, every word, phrase and exclamation mark she felt so deep inside her soul. As she wondered and guessed if his words do this to me, oh the magic he will lay across my body as he writes his next piece on his newly claimed canvas.

HER PLAYGROUND

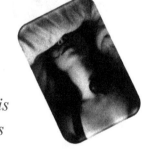

She slowly whispered in ear "My body his is your playground," oh playtime took on a whole new meaning.

CLUSTER OF GALAXIES

HER EYES A CLUSTER
OF GALAXIES
BREATHTAKINGLY
BEAUTIFUL
RADIATING SMILE
THAT EVEN THE
STARS DARE TO
COMPETE.
COSMIC
DUST SPRINKLED BARE
SKIN BUT JUST LIKE
THOSE STARS, HER LIGHT
SLOWLY DYING. WHAT FEW
DO NOT REALIZE IS A STAR'S
LIGHT DIMS RIGHT BEFORE IT
EXPLODES.

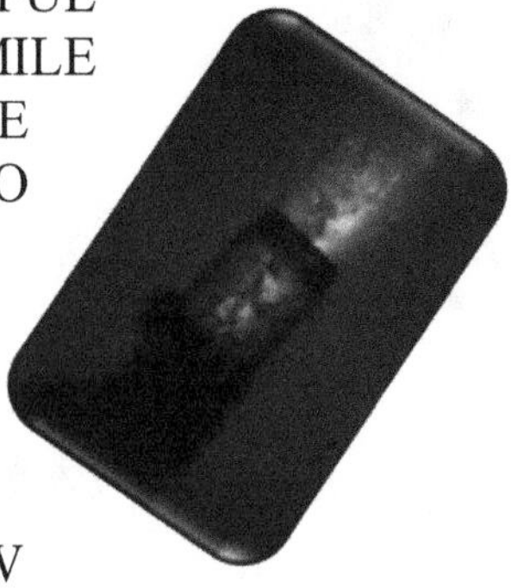

MOONLIGHT KISSES

*MOONLIGHT KISSES ON HER
HAIR, STARDUST SPRINKLED ON
SKIN SO BARE. MY CHANCES
NO MORE WITH EACH PASSING
STARE, HER EYES CASTING
ONLY GALAXIES AND BRIGHT
SOLAR FLARES.*

WILDFLOWER

She is too
wild for some, outspoken without
care; craziness is what she's become.
Wildflowers grow in her soul,
carelessness in her eyes, having others
believing there is no control. A goddess
like she; can never be caged, she will live forever free.

TOUCHING HER BODY

Do not touch my body for my body.
No touch me like no one has before.
Do not kiss my lips like all the rest.
Use your eyes as I use mine. Kiss my
broken heart, strip away all my doubts. Rip away all these
flaws, my insecurities I want them gone. Make passionate
love to my soul, however; if
telling you is what I must do,
then what is the point you will
not be true.

KEEPER

SHE DANCES UNDER THE
MOONLIGHT, NEVER
FEELING MORE ALIVE. HE
SAW THE STARS IN HER
EYES, IT WAS SOMETHING
SHE COULD NOT DISGUISE. GODDESS LIKE
FEATURES, HE KNEW SHE WAS A KEEPER.

SHE DESERVED BETTER

No one is perfect and everyone makes mistakes...I know I definitely have. My biggest mistake, greatest regret will forever be letting the absolute perfect, most amazing girl fall out of love with me. I now sit here today regretting all the things I could have done differently. I can say this, she taught me so much about myself that I never knew and that I will be forever grateful for. As I sit here today with all

this pain and heartache, I know she has moved on and found someone new. I just truly hope that he is treating her like the princess she was to me.... No he better be treating her like the queen I failed to treat her like.

LONELY STARS

Lonely stars shine as bright as the
gaze in her eyes, captivating and
true as the midnight skies.
Damaged broken and blue, love
will always be pursued.
Loving her would be a challenge she
warned, it is not for the faint of heart.
With such a simple kiss, finally finding
her sweet bliss

HER FIRE

SHE WAS FIRE, A HINT OF
TROUBLE, IN HER WORLD OF
CHAOS AND LOVE, BUT DAMN
THAT SMILE, HER SMILE CAST
ITS SPELL ON MY SOUL THAT
DARED ME TO LET HER IN.

HER KARMA

One day the girl that got away walked right in his path putting her Karma into play. My god it is the very man I left like he was nothing, I even laughed when he spoke of death. He must be doing amazing and I am over here in sweats and a pizza stain on my shirt. He  *remembered my name I am in shock. We spoke of times past, always able to make me laugh. As we parted ways I stood there in shame and disgust, that man was the only one to have ever loved me for me. I was once his princess. I left him that day absolutely no word to explain, I wish now I would have tried harder for that man to save me when I was once a slave.*

SMILE GONE

As I saw one day, I noticed her smile was gone, the sparkle all but disappeared now. Seeing this made me cry it is not who she is, it is not who I remember her as. There was such amazing love between us, the fire, the passion, and my god the connection. Few people will ever experience that raging hot fire and I got to and the burns will forever remind me of the passion we once shared.

SO, DID YOU

A friend asked me the other day, so did you love her, like really love her. Half a smile came to be as flashes of fond memories, the late-night laugh for no reason, to her cute thing when I would tell her things in Spanish, the endless staring into each other's eyes. Then a different set began to play, the always missing each other, time difference dislikes, waking up while I was still in bed, constant missing each other due to kids ruling her house, to she would be going to bed I was still up running around. Shaking these memories off made me really think, replying, yes, I loved her with all my heart, we were just passing through life kind of destined to be. I

will say this though she did teach me two most valuable lessons, she taught me how to be a better man and to absolutely love myself.

TWO LOST SOULS

Enter in two lost and damaged souls, knowing nothing but heartache and pain. Never have been loved before, the type of love that transforms. Molding your soul letting it intertwine with your body. Fate already had her plan that these two lost and unloved hearts would meet by sudden chance a lesson unlike any other was at hand. Forged before time this profound love a true masterpiece, sadly though it is not meant to last. These two wounded souls need to learn a lesson, a lesson of self-love. Never knowing how to absolutely love themselves this forged love will fix all their damaged and shattered parts. Finally having the lesson down, time had come for this amazing captivating love to end, cause their true love and forever soulmates will be introduced in their next chapter.

HER BLUE EYES

Just like that one beautiful day, I noticed this girl approaching my way. As she proceeded to say I do not mean to bother you but are you ok. Wondering why I would not be ok, explaining myself she stated no your eyes they are so dark. Throwing me off, explaining that I had a difficult past that they must now reflect all that pain I now carry. As tears formed, I told her not to cry, because it would cloud her stunning bright blue eyes. As she began to smile and blush, I told her maybe the reason why she approached me was it was destined for her bright blue eyes to finally clear my raging storm.

PARAGRAPH

YOU ONCE SAID YOU WANTED TO BE IN ALL REMAINING CHAPTERS IN THE BOOK OF MY SO-CALLED LIFE. I REALIZED TODAY THAT COULD NEVER HAPPEN TO SOMEONE WHO WAS MERELY A PARAGRAPH IN AN UNFINISHED CHAPTER OF MY LIFE.

SANDCASTLE

*YOU HAVE NEVER SEEN ME
CRUMBLE AND BREAK, ONE DAY
YOU WILL, AND I HOPE YOU
STAY, BECAUSE IT CAN
GET SCARY TO WATCH
SOMEONE FALL APART
AND DISINTEGRATE LIKE
A SANDCASTLE.*

SHE'S THE TYPE

*She is the type to dance in the rain with no
care who is watching. She loves the dark
standing under the moon. She will never fit in
with any of the crowds and that does not*

*bother her she is her own
crowd. Captivating eyes like
the stars in the sky, yet at the
same time she can use them
for your demise. A smile like
no other can lead you into a
hypnotized state or cast a spell
when you do her wrong leaving
you tormented for years to come.*

JUST WALK AWAY

SOMEONE TOLD ME TO JUST WALK AWAY, HOW DO YOU JUST WALK AWAY FROM SOMEONE YOU STILL LOVE. MEMORIES THAT WE SHARED, LOVE THAT WE GAVE STATING WE WOULD ALWAYS BE THERE. PICTURES NO LONGER ON MY WALLS, THE IMAGES STILL HAUNT ME, NOW MY VERY NIGHTMARES. ALWAYS ON MY MIND, STILL WONDERING IF YOU'RE FINE. HOW DOES ONE WALK AWAY FROM THAT, THE PROBLEM IS YOU NEVER WILL. SHE IS NOW EMBEDDED IN MY SOUL, FRAGMENTS OF HERS RIP AT MY HEART. MAYBE ONE DAY ALL OF THIS WILL DISAPPEAR, BUT MY LOVE FOR HER WILL ALWAYS BE THERE.

CHASED AWAY THE DARK

DARKNESS ALL AROUND, NEVER WANTING TO BE FOUND. TOUCHING HIS SOUL, THIS FEELING HE'S NEVER KNOWN. HER SMILE ALONE CHASED AWAY THE DARK THAT HE ONCE SWAM SO FREELY IN.

A SOUL SLOWLY DYING

DARKNESS ALL AROUND, EVERYONE WATCHING AS HE SLOWLY DROWNS. HIS MADE-UP SMILES ONLY FOOLED FOR A WHILE. IF ONLY YOU WOULD SEE INTO HIS EYES, ONLY THEN HIS SOUL YOU'LL SEE DYING.

SIMPLY POETIC

SOMEONE ONCE SAID, I ABSOLUTELY LOVE HOW A POET PUTS WORD TO PAPER WHICH MADE  *ME THINK. WHEN WE WRITE ARE WE WRITING FOR THEM, FOR THE READERS THAT ADMIRE EVERY WORD THAT WE SHARE. ARE THE WORDS BEING SAID, AND WRITTEN FOREVER IN INK, OUR OWN ESCAPE FROM THE VIOLENT STORMS IN OUR HEAD. TO WRITE DOWN HOW I FEEL IN WORDS, SO OTHERS MAY*  *UNDERSTAND ALL MY SECRET HIDDEN PAIN, WELL NOW THAT TO ME IS SIMPLY POETIC.*

BRAVE FACE

I have put on my brave face; I still want to believe you would not want me sad. Pushing you and our memories to the back of my mind, knowing dormant they will not stay. Like a summer storm blowing in, an image of you surfaced.

Waves of emotions slamming into my soul, like sheets of that rain. Tears run down  my face; no this is not supposed to happen. I am replaying that day over in my head, how could you of all people do it so freely. With that same storm it changed so quickly, how is this the same girl who absolutely loved me, once your prince I was your always to my forever. Storm subsided tears slowly drifting, just as fast as this mid-summer storm, our love disappeared with it. A smile slowly forming, like the sun emerging from once gray clouds. I will be good just as long as I know that somewhere out there you are happy and loved.

FOR TANISHA

She is always there when I finally crack and break. She is the one to pick me up in the wake of your destruction. Never asking questions, not even judging. Listening to me cry and beg for answers, feeling so helpless but always knowing the exact words to say. Never will I be able to thank her enough or begin to repay her, I just hope she knows exactly what she means to me and the love I have for her is the purest of all.

HER PLACE

Take her to a place she has only read about. Touch her so she feels it in her heart. Make love to her soul making her forget she was ever hurt. Strip away her insecurities showing her a side she is never seen. Pin her flaws to the wall slowly kissing away all the years of sadness and pain.

FINDING WORDS

FINDING WORDS TO DESCRIBE MY LOVE FOR YOU WILL NEVER BE ENOUGH BUT I WILL ALWAYS FIND THE RIGHT WORDS TO TELL YOU JUST HOW MUCH I LOVE YOU.

MISS THANG

Calling her my stepdaughter doesn't sound right, yeah she doesn't have my eyes, she doesn't have my hair, she'll never have my last name, but I can say this she stole my heart from day one. She may only be my stepdaughter, but I will always see her as my daughter. I love you Miss Thang

UNDER THE MOON

And under the moon so captivating and true, her beauty unlike no other, running through and through. Stars in her eyes ever so bright, leaving one's soul ready to ignite.

HIS DEPRESSION

Battling depression is a constant storm in your head, like an ocean of waves, slowly makes your soul decay. Like a sunken ship tormented with fierce waves, stripping all your layers away. The darkest of

nights, you do not have to always fight. Unlike like that sunken ship, your fierce ocean does not have to take ownership. Fighting your violent waves, sending your demons straight to their graves.

Forever Broken

My heart, fragile like glass, has been shattered by memories of the past. The pieces are scattered, jagged running with blood staining the ground. Two pieces are missing never to be found, the rest may never be stitched back together. I did not realize it for quite some time, those unnoticeable fragments gone forever; today not a smile nor laughter ever happen. The thread binding me together was ripped apart, and I was left holding shattered pieces of my heart. Will anyone help me fit it again? All it takes is love for it to mend, but the truth of the matter will make one sad, love is something I will never have. To this world I do not matter, my heart now will forever remain shattered.

NEVER BE ASHAMED

NEVER BE ASHAMED OF YOUR PAST, ALL THOSE MISTAKES CAN BE SURPASSED. ALL THE THOUGHTS BINDING AND COMPELLING. LEAVING ONE IN PAIN CONSTANT DWELLING. SHACKLES BINDING EVER SO TIGHT. YOUR MIND IS NOW FREE TO END THE TORMENTING FIGHT.

INTERTWINED

INTERTWINED IN HIS MIND; HIS DAILY THOUGHTS RAGED A WAR, STRIPPING AND SHAKING TO ITS CORE. SILENT SCREAMS CONTINUE THE FAKE SMILES, NOTHING MORE THAN ANOTHER TRIAL. THIS TIME HOWEVER, THE DEMONS WILL BE FOREVER DEAD TO ME.

HER MAGIC

She is the magic you only read about in books; her fire inside always misunderstood. Goddess like eyes so captivating leaving one mesmerized, will cast a spell leaving you so tantalized. Creatures like these, never meant to be tamed; she will live her life unconstrained.

UNKNOWN LOVE

LOVING YOU IS LIKE NO OTHER. YOU FELL FOR ME BEFORE WE TOUCHED, WRAPPING YOURSELF AROUND MY SOUL; AT LONG LAST YOU MADE ME WHOLE. MAKING LOVE WITH OUR WORDS, KISSING ME WITH YOUR GENTLE TOUCH; NEVER KNOWING THERE WAS A LOVE AS SUCH. STAR CROSSED LOVERS DESTINED TO BE, WRITTEN BEFORE OUR TIME; SOULMATES ARE FOUND ONCE IN A LIFETIME.

DARKNESS YOU CANNOT SEE

DARKNESS YOU CANNOT SEE,
DEMONS ALL AROUND LIKE
SCREE. DRAINING WITHIN MYSELF,
MY SOUL DYING IN ITSELF.
DEMONS DANCING WITH GLEE,
RUNNING RAMPANT SO
CAREFREE. CONTROL WAS LOST,
THAT FINE LINE HAS NOW BEEN CROSSED. TAKING
BACK CONTROL, MY SOUL WILL AGAIN BE ABSOLUTE
AND WHOLE.

MY LONELY ROAD

This lonely road
walking alone, it is all
I have ever had, all I
have ever known.
Silence deafening all
around, in my
darkness I slowly
drown.

MY SEVEN REASONS WHY

My story is far from over, I have so much more that needs to be told. You only heard the bad, now let me tell you of the good, the amazing and yet so sad. I have seven wonderful  *reasons why I am alive today. Reason #1 has its own amazing journey full of heartache, disappointment, joy, and fear, but it too has a wonderful tale. Now reason #2 is like no other full of grief and despair but unfolds with an unexpected twist that continues with wonder. Reason #3 however has a story unlike me for it has seen more demons and all before page #3. Reason #4 is full of joy and jokes that only two special people would know, for it is unlike any other cheer. Reason #5 has a surprise for this one has no disguise for it shows itself unlike no one else, full of laughs and even sad, but you'll be shocked by the chapter that follows because reason #6 would have never been if it weren't for some unfortunate*  *events all because it was already written that this special reason would be all that was needed to twist this tale to perfect but don't get me wrong this reason almost never was due to this stories main villain. Reason #6 fought like hell for its amazing now perfect part. We come to the final reason and so unique this reason will be. Reason #7 is like no other because it was brought in from another tale, a tale*  *of wonder and so much love. Reason #7 would become part of this amazing adventure, for it was brave and so perfect in its existence that it had their own chapter it needed to blossom and grow, we will get back to that. Now you have heard all seven reasons why I am alive today. Because of these amazing and wonderful yet individually unique reasons. Reason #1 has a name she goes by Ashley. She is my oldest most amazing beautiful, yet Loren is her first name, claiming she looks more like an Ashley so that is her name and she prefers it that way. Growing up without her father, regardless our history she loves me unconditionally. Reason #2 is my oldest son Andru, like his dad his first name is David, Andru has seen death and grief with his*  *mother's untimely death. Andru is so unique as well as strong never showing such pain, never falling apart. However, Reason #3 who has a close story to his older brother, Xzavier rarely falls apart, he too has his own demons that he fights just like his brother and dad. We welcome Reason #4 who is full of laughter and jokes because Alexander has his own creative mind. He and his dad will make you laugh till you cry like father like son. Down to Reason #5 this guy is Kyler not Tyler this little guy has such a mind he can make anything exciting and fun you should see him when he gets going behind his PC. Nickname is Monkey from his dad their bond is quite different, but his dad loves all his 7 reasons in their own unique ways. Reason #6 will surely make you cry because this little guy Hunter Dean has a very different tale, our series of events all due in part to an evil addiction that almost cost all the reasons to completely fall apart. Hunter's daddy was fighting a battle, addiction shackled such*  *a tight hold. The little miracle nicknamed Monster made this twist in our tale turning everything around, Hunter wants all to hear his chapter which we will come back to. Finally, this unique part that was brought into this addition Reason #7 introducing Lindsay Ann or as she has been known to answer to Miss Thang. She is my stepdaughter, I do not see her as such, due all in part to have raised her since the age of 3. She will never have my eyes, nor will she have my last name, but none of that matters I am seeing only a bright beautiful girl who stole my heart right from the start. So, there you have it, you have now heard of my seven reasons of why I am alive today for this new man can finally and forever be the dad they wanted and needed. Nothing and no one can or will ever break this new forged bond. I would not change anything not even the first sentence in this sad yet utterly amazing tale of my painful yet wonderful story of my life. My story is far from over......*

AFTER ALL

AFTER ALL I HAVE BEEN THROUGH, I HONESTLY DO NOT FEAR FALLING IN LOVE AGAIN. I MEAN THERE ARE A LOT OF THINGS I LOVE NOW. I LOVE MY CHILDREN. I LOVE BEING GOOFY AND WEIRD. I LOVE THE SMELL OF NEWLY FALLEN RAIN. I LOVE LAYING OUT ON A SUMMER'S NIGHT GAZING AT THE STARS NO

CARES IN THE WORLD. I MAY EVEN FALL IN LOVE AGAIN SOMEDAY. I AM NOT AVOIDING IT, BUT WHAT I DO FEAR HOWEVER; IS FALLING LIKE I DO, SO DEEPLY AND PASSIONATELY HARD, INVESTING MY LIFE INTO THEIRS ONLY TO DISCOVER THEY NEVER FELT THE SAME, OR LYING ABOUT THINGS THEY HAD DONE. THIS IS HOW YOU DIE WHILE STILL BEING ALIVE AND IT IS A NIGHTMARE TRYING TO PULL YOURSELF OUT OF THAT HEARTACHE AND DEPRESSION. THE FACT OF THE MATTER IS, YOU TRULY ARE NEVER GOING TO KNOW WHO YOU ARE FALLING IN LOVE WITH UNTIL IT IS TOO LATE, NOW THAT RIGHT THERE IS MY BIGGEST FEAT.

THE UNIVERSE

THE UNIVERSE WILL BRING SOMEONE INTO OUR LIVES TO EITHER PASS THROUGH AND BE A LESSON OR ENTER OUR LIVES AND BE OUR FINAL LESSON.

SUCH PAIN

Not too many people in their lifetime will have to experience such pain. The type of pain from someone who said they loved you, would give the world to you, care for you without a second guess. Finally making you whole and absolute, only to have them turn their backs on you and pretend you never existed. Walking out of your life with no reasons why. Leaving you even worse than before. A stranger again but now your secrets in tow. Now that pain takes a lifetime to heal.

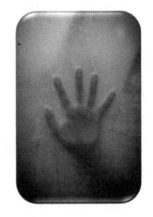

ONE CAN ONLY

*ONE CAN ONLY FAKE IT FOR SO
LONG. ONE CAN ONLY WEAR
THAT FAKE SMILE FOR SO
LONG. ONE DAY ALL OF
THAT WILL BECOME TOO
MUCH...HOLDING ON
FOR SO LONG, I
HAVE HAD ENOUGH
IT IS TIME FOR ME
TO BREAK.*

IMPRINTED

*LEAVING HER SOUL IMPRINTED UPON MINE,
SLOWLY DYING WHILE
STILL ALIVE, OH BUT
WHAT BITTERSWEET
AGONY IT WILL BE.*

THERE COMES A TIME

There comes a time in your life when you are just done. Done with the pain that drains the life from you every minute of every day. Some may look at you as a coward for giving  *up, those are the ones that know nothing of this pain. Always smiling yet on the inside slowly dying, screaming for someone to hear and the ones you want to hear are no longer there. I hope that you will stop and see, on just how many lives you have touched. I know and have felt that pain I understand the storm that infest your brain. The thoughts are wrong that is what they want, consume and control even devour your mind. Trust me when I say, this storm does pass it will diminish. Do not be the writer to your end, lets fight together I got your back if you got mine.*

DOES THE PAIN GO AWAY?

Someone asked me, when does the pain go

away? oh, you poor thing this must be your first heartbreak. The truth of it is, that pain you feel deep down where her love once was, now a dark emptiness that will forever fill her void. The thoughts that keep you up at night. Those will forever haunt now your new nightmares. Yes, you will move on, think of her less; maybe if you are lucky the images will fade. Your wounds will heal, scars slowly fade away. With each passing day your heart begins to heal, that pain you asked of; it truly does finally go away. Memories are now but a distant past, that pain you asked of it, too will pass.

DEMON'S

IT IS THAT TIME OF THE NIGHT
WHEN THE DEMONS WANT TO
COME OUT AND DANCE IN MY
HEAD. TUGGING AND PULLING
LAUGHING WITH
JOY OF ALL PAST
MISTAKES.
HOWEVER THERE
COMES A TIME
WHEN ALL THAT
SHIT BACKFIRES,
LEAVING THEM
RUNNING FUCKING
SCARED. DO NOT TRY TO FUCK
WITH MY MASTER OF DISGUISE
THOSE WERE MY DARK TIMES
WHICH I AM NOW IN CONTROL
OF.

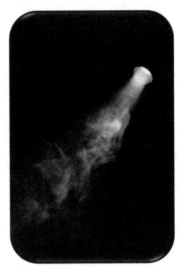

MOST WANT

MOST GUYS WANT THE TROPHY
WIFE. ALL DONE UP WITH NAILS
AND HAIR. ALWAYS DOING THINGS
THAT ARE SOCIALLY IN. THAT IS OK
FOR SOME, BUT NO ONE WILL EVER
WANT THAT AGAIN AFTER MEETING
A GIRL WHO LOVES THE DARK. ONE
WITH THE OUTSPOKEN MIND,
EXTREMELY LOVING
HEART. SHE COULD
HAVE HER ENTIRE
WORLD COLLAPSE
AROUND HER AND
WITHOUT ANY
THOUGHTS PICKS
HERSELF UP AND
WALKS IT OFF. WHY
WOULD ANYONE

WANT THE BORING SAME, WHEN A
GIRL OF DARK WILL NOT BLIND
YOU WITH SUCH TALES OF A
BETTER COMING. WHEN THIS GIRL
OF DARK KNOWS OF TRUE PAIN AND
SHE WILL BRACE THE STORM WITH
YOU FOR WHEN IT PASSES, SHE
WILL SHOW THE BEAUTY LEFT IN
ITS WAKE. A BEAUTIFUL GIRL WHO
LOVES THE DARK, SOUNDS
ABSOLUTELY BEAUTIFUL TO ME.

MINE

Wondering how she wore beautiful so well, what chance did

 I have when her eyes meet

with mine. My soul soon

mesmerized, captivating

blue eyes; her spell cast my heart forever in a trance.

Goddess like features yet my

attraction comes when our souls

slowly become one. Perfect in every

aspect of the word, could she be my

once in a lifetime. Slowly bending,

fusing to one; I can only hope she will

be my happily ever after.

ANOTHER LATE NIGHT

*It is these late nights when you cannot sleep
so you stare at your walls waiting for the
pain to go away. Slowly
feeling my soul decay
emptiness inside once
filled with a thing I
thought was love. It
was your pitch-dark
veil, covering all your lies
your deceit now covers my heart.
Our love unlike any other igniting what I
believed was an endless flame, once burnt
hotter than a solar flame. Just like the
universe you managed to cause our flame to
slowly die out. The lies exploding like a
dying star, the trust I once had gone in a
flash with a shower meaningless hateful
word. Unlike your idea of love, the love that
once burned for your soul will never go out,
it was always meant to guide you through the
dark. Blinded today without your flame I
hope the darkness will forever dissipate.*

SOMETHING INSIDE

Something inside like no other, making your heart skip and flutter. Star crossed lovers forever destined, your soul will not be left guessing. Ever so sweet butterfly kisses, that long-lost piece; no longer missing. Souls colliding and bonding as one, passion burning hotter than the sun. Today finally complete, marveling in fates masterpiece.

FOREIGN LOVE

SHOWING LOVE WAS SECOND NATURE TO HER, LIKE A PERSON WHO SPEAKS THEIR OWN LANGUAGE. YET AT TIMES SHE STUMBLED AS A PERSON TRYING TO SPEAK A NEW LANGUAGE.

WHAT I HAVE TO OFFER

I KNOW YOU HAVE BEEN TO HELL, HAD YOUR HEART BROKEN AND LEFT IN PIECES. TATTERED AND TORN BY SO MANY BEFORE. I DO NOT HAVE A LOT; I CANNOT EVEN BUY YOU FANCY THINGS. I CAN GIVE YOU SOMETHING EVEN GREATER, I CAN GIVE YOU A LOVE THAT YOU HAVE NEVER HAD BEFORE. THOSE ONCE BROKEN PIECES, IF YOU WILL LET ME, I WILL PUT YOUR HEART BACK TOGETHER SO THAT THEY WILL FIT PERFECTLY WITH MINE AND OH WHAT A LOVE WE WILL FOREVER SHARE.

THE BREAKUP

Today I finally stood up, haunting memories no more of that breakup. Your essence still upon my lips, even after my soul you so violently stripped. This is not the person I wish to become; with  *all you have done could I really expect a different outcome. You said you loved me but that was a lie, still to this day I wonder why. You watched me stumble, you watched me break; looking back down you were another horrible mistake. I thank you because you made me a better person, but I hate you for draining me, you gave him your while I gave you mine. Trusting no longer comes as easy, my love I will never again give so freely. If my next love should come around, I will make sure before it starts to fucking burn it all down.*

SUPERNOVA

Like a cosmic storm a million pieces of both, spinning so fierce their souls now denote. Particles of sorrow, dusting of heartbreak; rainbows of sadness slowly take it shape. Like a star being born, the sight so adorns. Binding and molding coming together as one, we watch their love finally take its form. Their love like the material to birth a star, forming and molding their new love is now

adhering. However just like a burning star, it does not last forever; their flame of love will slowly die until none. The love they shared now foregone, all their material that brought them as one. Exploding from their inside, throwing all their particles and materials back into the world; this sad yet amazing site happens more than you think when once true love goes supernovae.

FALL IN LOVE WITH ONLY WORDS

As she sat and watched his mind wonder, her very own drifted away. She remembered all that he told, how his heart had been tattered and torn. Such loving captivating words that he writes, every letter and phrase touches and caresses my body. As I read all that he writes, I feel his words exploring

like no other. Every sentence as they pass, he steals my breath without lips ever touching. Confused by what he once said, tears forming each one for all that they did. His words now lay upon my body our love binding as such, years of torment and pain now erased with her love breaking its once evil clutch.

I WILL TAKE ALL THE BLAME

*Today was my final break, pain, and
heartache I will no longer take.
Everyone before now I am counting
you, all walked out of my life I was a
miscue. Never thinking or pondering
the pain, heartless and selfish they all
managed to throw me the blame. The*

*person I am took it in stride, little did any of them know all
those nights I just laid there and cried. Do not begin to*

*question the man who stands before you
today, all your heartless acts finally have
consumed me with darkness
and dismay. Slowly they will begin to
remember and regret, never did forget
destroying your feelings I am dead set.
Stooping to your level I will not go; your
time will come my pain you will know.*

WORDS OF SUCH CARE

AS I LAY HERE REPLAYING MY NOT TOO DISTANT PAST, MEMORIES THAT MAKE ME LAUGH; THEN THE ONES THAT ESCAPE I WILL NEVER HAVE. TEARS STREAMING BEFORE I EVEN REALIZE, THIS TIME HOWEVER THINGS ARE UNIQUELY DIFFERENT. SOFTLY AND SLOWLY THEY BEGIN TO FADE AWAY, NO LONGER YOUR IMAGE SET ON REPLAY. WHO IS THIS SLOWLY COMING INTO FOCUS, SUCH BEAUTY NOW FILLING MY ONCE CLOUDED EYES? MY HEART SHATTERED SCATTERED AT MY FEET; SHE CANNOT SEE THIS RECENT

DEFEAT. FRANTICALLY TRYING TO GATHER THE PIECES, CUTS AND SCRATCHES THE BLOOD NOW STAINING WITHOUT CARE. SLOWLY KNEELING, HER WORDS WITH SUCH CARE; CALMS MY FEARS AND TELLS ME SHE IS NOW THERE.

NEVER LOVED

NEVER HAVE YOU MADE ME FEEL LOVED, LEAVING ME WONDERING IF I WAS EVER ENOUGH. SECRETS AND LIES CLOUDING YOUR MIND, HEART AND SOUL ARE NOW DISINCLINED. AS IT SLOWLY CONSUMES YOU WHOLE, ALL AT ONCE YOU LOSE CONTROL. YOUR LIES AND TALES START TO UNWIND, WATCHING THIS DOWNFALL SHE IS THE MASTERMIND. THINKING OF ONLY YOURSELF, THE FAKE LOVE I HAVE NOW EXPELLED. COVERING MY EYES WITH YOUR EVIL DECEIT, THIS TIME YOUR LIES HAVE BEEN FOR SEEN. YOUR GAME IS UP FINALLY REVEALED, ALL YOU HAVE DONE NOW WALK YOUR OWN BATTLEFIELD.

WORDS UPON MY BODY

As she whispers in his ear, of all the things she will endear. Touching her body slowly kissing her secret places, not with touch his words across her body he now traces. Her body now his newfound playground, playtime like never before; new rules today her body now wants to be pinned down. Shallow breathing with every touch, never has words ever done such. His words slowly have been laid, my body his living canvas; the love we made will never fade; such beautiful words will never fade.

BEAUTIFUL DREAM

You are a dream that was once trapped in my mind, the inner workings the universe has yet to intertwine. I have dreamt of your essence, never knowing your existence. Hearing you speak with such care, wondering if my demons will leave you scared. Thoughts of your tender touch, doubts clouding leaving me wondering if I even deserve that much. Picking up everything broken from time, my wall ever so high as I marveled as she climbed. Could this be the one set me free, loving every damaged and shattered piece of me.

ALONE

ALWAYS ALONE NEVER REALLY ANYONE'S GO TO IF THEY ONLY KNEW THE STRUGGLES I SILENTLY VIEW. PAIN AND TORMENT CLAW AWAY A SILENT MONSTER SECRETLY TUCKED AWAY. ON MY OUTSIDE LAUGHTER AND JOKES FILL YOUR EARS, MY DEMONS AND THOUGHTS WOULD BRING YOU NOTHING BUT TEARS. ALWAYS FIGHTING THIS NEVER-ENDING BATTLE, SUCH PAIN HAS RIPPED AND SKINNED MY VERY SOUL AWAY. YOU MAY SEE ME CRUMBLE, YOU MAY SEE ME BREAK; BUT THIS BATTLE YOU WILL NEVER SEE ME BACK AWAY FROM.

CAN YOU LOVE ME?

Love me like no one has before, show me why people search out this love. What is it used for, do even know what it does? Feelings surge through your soul, can you describe some more.

Feelings of butterflies you claim things as such, do you think my soul is just dead. Never have I felt these feelings you speak of, perhaps I am broken unlovable even. I have been told this word before, yet you say when the words are said I would know if it was truly meant.

Forever I will wonder around in search of this love, maybe it is my fate a broken

person unworthy. A soulmate I heard is the one worthy of, unlocking this love even setting my soul ablaze. Why would someone want a broken and damaged unlovable mess? As she gently placed her hand upon his chest, her voice intoxicating; "I love this broken and damaged mess." Everything about this man is perfect, even all his imperfect flaws.

Loving this man the moment my eyes spotted him, hearing a soft faint whisper "oh there he is..my perfectly imperfect soulmate now our adventures can begin,"

SUNFLOWERS

There is the girl with sunflowers in her eyes, been through such a violent past you would never tell covering it so well. View the world as she sees, delicate words run through her soul. Perfectly imperfect along with her damaged soul, stops at nothing to explore another just like her. Like a beautiful spring day as rain beings to descend, will always find her

dancing for its her best friend. So many years searching for a perfect imperfect to finally match and bond all her perfectly laid out flaws. And when these two finally meet, a imperfectly perfect bond will forever keep.

DOUBTING

Seeing you doubting yourself, I too once always second guessed myself. The way you carry all that weight, the burdens those shoulders hold I too have known. Always putting yourself down, if only you could see yourself through the world's eyes. Giving in to those demons it is their game they play, once so loud now silenced are mine yours too will get along someday. Do not give in the mind it plays such evil tricks, like a cancer they cannot stay forever affixed. My wings I will give so you can learn to fly, away from this gray higher till your demons you defy.

Fear and uncertainty, I know that look of depreciation, a new belief you will find in yourself; the road less traveled is now your destination.

SIREN

 *HER CARING WORDS THAT OF A SIREN,*

SOOTHING AND CALMING TRICKING THE

DEMONS; WAVES OF FALSE LOVE

SO TANTALIZINGLY. HER VENOM SLOWLY

INJECTED, SILENTLY YET SWIFT HER NEXT

VICTIM YOU BECOME; EVERYTHING AND EVERYONE YOU

ONCE LOVED ALL BUT GONE NOW EXACTLY AS

SHE EXPECTED. WEB OF CONTROL MANIPULATING YOUR

EVERY THOUGHT, TANGLED MESS OF LIES MIXED WITH

FALSE LOVE EVEN HOPE, HER

FINAL KILL TACIT DESPERATE

ONSLAUGHT. VENOM SUBSIDIES

HER NIGHTMARE UNREALISTIC, THE

WOMAN I ONCE LOVED I CARED FOR SO MUCH, REALITY OF

THE MATTER I HAD JUST BEEN CONSUMED AND

CONTROLLED BY A NARCISSISTIC.

SOMEONE ELSE

I gave you my all while you were
worried about someone else. The day
to day making sure you were ok,
always reminding you to eat, at the
time finding it cute truth be told you
forgot because you were more
worried about someone else. Always
on my mind, as you heartlessly feed
me lies. Yes, the day will come as you

sit and look and finally see all the fucking damage you caused
me. Endless night countless tears, my fucking feelings you now
had new fears. Torn between a man who absolutely loved you,
and a controlling narcissistic man who truly only used you.
Chances gone love I finally fucking burnt that shit. That day
will come hitting you with the force of a million tons. Maybe
that day you will see my defeat, the guilt alone knocking you
off your feet. All my fucking pain will swarm and decay you
once good pure heart. As I sit here thinking of all
that agony and such deep fucking pain, no I
do not wish that upon you; I am a
man who once loved that pure heart.
Emptiness will consume you
and only then will know how
I felt when you left with my
heart that day

CRAVINGS

TO CRAVE A TOUCH,
YOU HAVE NEVER FELT
OR A KISS YOU HAVE YET
TO EXPERIENCE.
CAN TWO PEOPLE REALLY
BE CONNECTED IN A WAY NO ONE CAN DESCRIBE,
HAD ALL OF THIS ALREADY INSCRIBED. WALKING
INTO YOUR LIFE REGARDLESS OF TIME OR DISTANCE,
FEELING THE SOUL TUGGING AND PULLING TOWARDS
THE OTHER SO MUCH
INSISTENCE. THEY SAY
WHEN TWO PEOPLE HAVE
BEEN FORGED AND
FUSED SO LONG AGO, THE
UNIVERSE WILL DO ITS
ALL TO SEE THESE
UNBREAKABLE SOULS
THOUGH

INTOXICATING

SO FAMILIAR YET I
HAVE ONLY JUST
LEARNED HER NAME,
HOW CAN A SIMPLE

WORD CROSS MY LIPS, INTOXICATING MY SOUL
SETTING MY HEART AFLAME. EVERY SINGLE LETTER
EXQUISITE AS THE NEXT, MY SOUL NOW
FULLY INTOXICATED, LEAVING ME LOST AND VEXED.
HER BEAUTY AS CAPTIVATING AS A SETTING SUN, A
VOICE THAT CAN PLACE ONE IN A TRANCE; MY SOUL

FULLY DRUNK OFF HER
NAME NEVER DO I WISH
THIS UNDONE.

DO DREAMS COME TRUE?

DO DREAMS REALLY COME
TRUE, HAS FATE STEPPED IN
A PLAN I MUST CONSTRUE.
MYSTERIOUS WITH GODDESS
LIKE FEATURES, ALL THAT
HAVE APPROACHED NOTHING
BUT DREAMERS. HER PERSON
SHE WILL FIND, HEARTS OF PAST
DAMAGE SOON TO BE ALIGNED.
FORCES OF UNKNOWN SUCH AS
THAT IN THE UNIVERSE, TWO
LOST SOULS FINALLY CONVERSE.
NEVER ANY MEETING,
EXPLANATION VOID,
FINALLY
TOGETHER BACK
AS ONE WITH
EACH OTHER THEY
ARE KEEPING.

ABOUT THE AUTHOR

David Vidales in his follow up to "My Dark Wonderland" used recent personal trials, and tragedies to his advantage. To fight through his depression, he once again picked up a pen. Compared to his debut "My Dark Wonderland" with recent tragedies his writing style drastically changed. He fought and won against his demons, now through his words he wrote in that tough time again he wants others to know it does not last forever, there is a light at the end. To find out more visit his website at www.darkwonderlandpoetry.com also on Facebook @darkwonderlandpoet. He is currently a student at M.C.C working towards his bachelor's degree in Substance Abuse Counseling.

CPSIA information can be obtained
at www.ICGtesting.com
Printed in the USA
LVHW082103080920
665324LV00001B/3